JOY OF THE CARIBBEAN

Trevor East

GW00543995

ARTHUR H. STOCKWELL LTD
Torrs Park, Ilfracombe, Devon, EX34 8BA
Established 1898
www.ahstockwell.co.uk

British Library Cataloguing-in-Publication Data.
A catalogue record for this book is available
from the British Library.

ISBN 978-0-7223-4242-8
Printed in Great Britain by
Arthur H. Stockwell Ltd
Torrs Park   Ilfracombe
Devon EX34 8BA

CONTENTS

THE MASTERFUL

Love, the blindest of them all,
The most refreshing and exalted of them all,
The most powerful and strongest of them all.

With three streams it lies,
If power, kindness, happiness and joy.

Like water, it quenches the thirst;
Like fire, it burns the mind;
And like blood, it serves the heart;
Like the sun, it brightens and glorifies.

And, like the darkness,
It hides and quiet thing.
Love the masterful –
The power for the powerless.

THE LOVE OF MUM

When I was born,
She held me tight in her arms.
She comforted me; she kept me warm.

She cried her tears;
The sorrow she did bear.
But most of all, I was not aware
How much she did care.

And on the day I took my first step,
I fell, I fear,
But my mum was there
To show her love – how much she care!

She took me up in her arms
And comforted me so tenderly.

THE PASSION

The passion of love,
And dreams to remember when I die.
My friends and folks will gather and cry.
In my thoughts I wonder why.

'Am I a king or just another guy?'
I asked myself, but the answer won't come by.
I stand there and watch the people cry.

In my heart I wave them goodbye.
I wander off to a place where I can't tell why –
A secret which no one can ever know or tell.

A place of happiness or disaster?
No one can ever tell.
The freedom of mine can never compare.
If I die, I'll ask myself the question 'Why?'

THE TWO MOST
WONDERFUL PEOPLE TO HAVE

Mum and Dad are the two most wonderful people to have.

Mum she always makes me have.
And so with dad:
He always makes me glad.

In her arms she holds me tight
And comforts me all through the night.
With Mum and Dad I always have.

They make me glad
When I am sad.
They bring me joy.
They buy me toys.
Mum and Dad: the perfect guides
For me to have.

GREEDY

If the truth is in you,
Then the Glory of God
Shall rise above us all
And the evil of man
Shall perish like the dust
Of the earth we walk upon.

What shall it profit me
To live in the place of hell
With all the riches and wealth,
Lust of the flesh
And greed for power?

My brothers, this is only a moment of happiness
In your castle of destruction, sorrow and woe.

My brothers, lift up yourselves
From the sorrow of darkness
And search for the light,
And the truth will satisfy your heart.
For the greed for power
Is a bellyful of destruction.

MY ROSE GARDEN

The feeling I have
And the love I cherish!
My darling, please let me be your gardener,
That I may water your garden in the summer
And flourish it in the spring.

Spring is a season
And also a liquid:
But the most beautiful
Season of all to me
Is the season spring.

And my liquid water,
Spring, is fresh
And water is pure;
So, my darling,
What more can you ask
From me but my
Loving heart and a life
Filled with happiness?

THE SHINING LIGHT

In the night, when the sun
Has lost his light,
I sit in the darkness
Whispering to the shadow
Of the night.

Desperately waiting for the moon
To give us his shining light,
I hear the creatures of the
Night singing joyful songs to
The twinkling stars that
Shine so bright.

Hours later, when the
Darkness loses its appetite,
I greet the sun,
With the brilliance of its
Shining light.

CHILDREN, TAKE HEED

Respect your parents,
For they were here before you.
Good parents restrain
Their child from wrongdoing.

The honour of a son brings
Glory to his parents,
And a daughter
Brings happiness to the
Heart of her mother
And welcome joy to the man
That chooses her for his wife.

Most of the time when
The morale of a man
Is down, it takes the
Strength and love of a
Woman to lift him up.

The honour and strength of
A man are based on the love and care
Of the woman he loves. He puts his
Faith and trust into the care of
The woman he loves.

To him she is like the star
That shines in the darkness
And the warmness that the
Summer brings. The love of
A woman is worth more than
The value of gold; and all
The world's riches cannot compare.

WHEN THE SUN GOES BY

In the night when the sun goes by
And the darkness covers the sky
I see the stars that twinkle
And share their light.

Around the moon they travel the sky.
In my heart I
Wonder why.

I sit in the distance
Overlooking the hill –
The hill that overlooks the mountain,
Where the clouds come down to lie.

In my eyes
Joy brings tears that make me cry,
The gift of love that passes us by,
Happiness and joy that will never die.

MY FRIEND

I am a servant
To my lover –
The joy that brings forth happiness.

I am a fountain
That keeps on flowing.
I am like a stream
That keeps on running.

I am a circle.
I am a ring.
I have no beginning.
I have no end.

I am a lover.
I am a friend.
I am near.
I am far.

I am close.
I am wide.
I am a light.
I cannot hide.

THE OCEAN'S CRY

Like a ship that sails
Across the blue Caribbean sea –
The tender love I share with thee.

In the night I listen to the ocean's cry;
In silence its word goes by.
Like a ship that sails on top of the ocean sea,
In the silence of the night
I sit and watch her float by.

As the sound of the wave hits the
Rock and the seashore I cover
Myself in the silence of
The night,
Wondering where I shall be
If only Love could take me in
Her arms and cover me
With happiness.

How long shall I wait to
See the time of joy,
When she conquers sorrow
And covers my heart
With the loving bride
Of happiness?

THE STANDING SHADOW

As I lie in my bed,
Holding up my pillow,
Watching the moonlight
Through the window.

As the stars gather themselves
And march around
The sky, group by group.

As the cloud whispers to
The standing shadow
As it passes by, thinking
Of the dawn that tomorrow
Shall bring.

As the peeping sunlight
Brightens the sky,
The darkness of the
Night slowly went by.

THE CHANGING OF TIME

If everything would change,
Make my love to be
The same, how happy it
Would be as two hearts
Beat the same!

How pleasant it would be,
The true love that I
Share with thee!

My heart is like a flowing
River that runs through
The centre of your body.
It is like a stream
That never runs dry.

It is a light that keeps
On shining. It is life.
It is strength. It endures.
It never ends.

MY MOTHER'S LOVE

Her heart is like true
Diamond; her love is like
Precious gold.
Like a mountain, she overlooks
The sea.

Like the valley, she hides
Beneath the hill. Like the
Stream, she runs to the
River. And like the river,
She flows to the sea.

And like the sea, she
Makes love to the ocean.
And like the ocean, she
Travels around the earth
And brings
Joy to the precious land.

The precious land interacts
With the sea and the sand
And brings joy to all
Loving humanity.

FREEDOM

Freedom, hear my cry.
Destiny is my name.
I was born and grew
In the Caribbean, in Jamaica.

This is where my story
Began. I walk the street,
I travel the land,
Like a sailing ship across
The rough ocean.

In the sea or on the
Land, destiny is what I am;
I am she, the motherland.
I am her, the foundation.

I am right, but you are wrong.
You are weak, but I am strong.
Destiny is what I am.
People say I am big and strong;
Who do you say that I am?

I am the sea, I am the sand,
I am the water, I am the land;
And where you stand
Is my foundation.
Destiny is what I am.

NATURE

Nature – the beauty of the earth.
I see the cloud below the sky
And the birds that fly so high.
I ask myself, 'Is it real?'

The beauty of the spring
And the welcome joy it bring –
I ask myself, 'Is it real?'

Heaven, hear my cry.
Down on earth I will abide.
I ask myself, 'Is it real?'

The thing I do sometimes is I tell.
The secret I keep I hide it well.
Beneath the earth is the
Pillow of darkness.

But, high above, the cloud goes round.
In the morn the sun breaks the dawn.
I ask myself, 'Is it real?'

I stand up high on my feet
To greet the sun
When the morning comes.
Lots of things we have to do
If only time could see me through.
I ask myself, 'Is it real?'

OH, DARLING

My darling, how long shall
I wait to see the beauty
Of your love shine through
My heart? My heart is longing
For the happiness which has avoided
Me for so long.

I am in the midst of loneliness.
For so long I have been
Searching. My darling, please help
Me to find what I need.

I am a lover, and what I need
Is love. I search to find what
Is mine. Seasons come and seasons go,
But in my heart my love continues to flow.

Like a child that's desperate to
Take his or her first steps,
On that day it brings joy to his
Or her heart and happiness to the
Delight of the mother.

She holds him or her up in her
Arms and hugs him or her so tight.
And with a kiss she says,
"Oh, my baby, you are so sweet!"

So, my darling, make me be the
One you hold so tight in your
Arms and comfort me with your love.

WILD FLOWER

Like a wild flower.
No one seems to notice
It grow in the garden
Among the thorns, so lonely
And cold
Until on the first day of spring,
When the bird and the bee
Come to visit.

She blooms so wonderful,
To the delight of the gardener.
He smiles and pampers her.

When the summer comes
Around she is watered and
Mulched and cared for gently;
So the wild flower among
The thorns becomes the beauty
Of the garden.

As the seasons pass, the wild
Flower grows in strength and
Honour, beauty and love. She flourishes
Among them all.

As seasons come and seasons go,
One year ends and the next begins,
One life lost and the next one
Found, but remember the gossip
Of life will never end. Where
One is lost a next one is found. Where one
Life is taken a next one is given.

MOTHER'S ARMS

The arm of a mother
Is so tender and sweet,
But the arm of my lover
Cannot compare to others,
Because love seems most beautiful
To those who deserve it most.

When the flower blooms it
Smells so sweet and looks
So beautiful; but for my darling,
Love and beauty will always
Be the same; nothing will
Ever change.

Oh, can I be lonely when
The beauty of your love surrounds
Me? My heart is full of happiness.
I shed tears of joy.

Happiness fulfils my heart
And sweeps away the tears of
Sorrow. Can a man be ashamed of
Love? And can a man refuse
Happiness?

Happiness is the pillow of
Joy, and joy brings forth
Comfort. So, my darling, your
Loving arm is my tenderness
And your true love brings
Forth happiness to my life.

LIKE THE BEAUTY OF YOUR SMILE

Like the sun that rises in the
Morning and the moon that shines
In the night,
The stars gather around the
Moon to show their welcome
Happiness.

Oh, wonderful is the breath of
Life that is given unto the body
Of man!

I walk the desert and throughout
The surrounding land.
Queens and princesses I have
Known, but the love and beauty
Of my heart I could not have found
In any other but you.

The beauty of my love rests
In your heart and love
And comfort lies in your
Arms. The shadow of doubt
Shall be no more.

It is like passing from one world to another,
Like changing life for death
And light for darkness.

MY FLOWER GARDEN

Please water my garden
With the drops of your tears
And make it flourish with the beauty
Of your smile.

Although I may be tempted by
The beauty of others, my love
For you is so true
That it will never die.

KNOWLEDGE

Seek knowledge and be
Happy. Happy are the happy heart.
Wise are the knowledge mind.
Pure are the loving ones.

Joyful hearts bring happiness.
Unity is solid strength.
Build your mind with solid love.
Strengthen your heart with happiness.

Teach the children while they are
Young, so they will grow with dignity.
Teach your children to remember
God, to accept gratefully the little
That they have.

In this world there are rich
And poor. God is the Maker
Of them all.

Some are big and some are small.
God is the Master of them all.
Show kindness to the weak.
God is the Judge of the meek.

ONLY GOD KNOWS IT ALL

In the night I pray to God
And thank Him for the little that I have.
So many things I want to do –
Only You can take me through.

God is good and God is great.
Only a few really appreciate.
As I wake from the morning break
I pray to God to give me faith.

He hears my prayer
He plans my date.
Listen to His trumpet
Before it's too late.

MAN, THE SUBSTANCE OF THE DUST

Man – what is man?
Man – who is man?
The image of God's own Self
Or the power of an Unseen Being?
Man – the shadow of the darkness
Or the power of the burning flame?

Man – the enemy of himself
Or the shadow of his cruelty?
Man – a danger to this world
Or the treasure of God's glory?

Man – who is man?
The image of his Father
Or the substance of the dust?
Man – can he change?

THE PURITY OF LOVE

Love is pure and so am I.
Love is true and so I do.
Love is not what you are,
But what you do.

Speak the truth and be yourself.
Love is everlasting and so am I.
I see the things I want to do,
But only love can take me through.

I spread my wings far and wide
Just to fly above the sky.
In the night my tears I cry.

Loneliness keeps standing by.
I ask myself the question 'Why?'
Oh, great God, hear my cry:
Give me the knowledge to understand why.

SATAN'S CHARIOT

The world is on
The chariot of Satan.
I need neither gold nor silver –
Only the precious love of God.

All the wealth and riches
Bring only a moment of joy.
Happiness and joy
Bring forth peace.

And with peace
I truly understand
What is happiness.

The breath of life
May be taken away,
But memory will
Always be here to stay.

MY LADY

My lady she is like
Paradise to me.
Her smile is so brilliant –
Like the rising sun on top
Of the blue mountain peak.

Her kiss is so sweet
That it gives me a slow heartbeat
Beneath the sky so high
And the clouds so low.

Only God in heaven can know
How much I love her so.
If strength is energy, and my sweat and tears show
How much I care –
How much love we share.

Now, my darling, have no fear –
All my love I will always share.
When I am far or even near
My tender heart will always be there
And my sparkling love I will always share.

THE BEAUTIFUL GARDEN

The beautiful garden
Man calls earth – how pleasant it
Would be to see the wonderful
Things that nature gives!

We are all creatures of our Master,
The King and Creator. I adore the
Beautiful things that life has to offer.

The most wonderful and
Precious Master made the birds,
The flowers and the trees, but
Most wondrous of all is the beautiful lady He
Made for me.

With lots of love and tender care,
The sorrow and joy we always share.

When I am down she lifts me up.
When I am weak she carries me.
She lifts me up in her arms.
She hugs me tight and keeps me warm.

Oh, my darling, you are the
Treasure in my arms
And the happiness to my heart.

THE GLORY OF LOVE

The glory of love is happiness,
And the truth brings forth freedom.
Never be a prisoner to yourself
Or a slave to your own mind.

Like the moon that glorifies
The night, the sun
Breaks the shade of day.

I watch the seasons go by.
Winter is when I was in my mother's womb;
Spring is when I was a newborn child.
In summer I became so warm and happy.
With strength I grew and was glorified with love.

Then came autumn. I grow old,
My strength fails, and my body
Wither away and fall like leaves
And become mulch.

But the love of my heart
Shall never fall in memories.
It shall live on for evermore.

MY DARLING

My darling, remember me
When you are in distress.
My love is like a shield
That guides and protects you
Through the shadow of the darkness
In the night.

I send my shield to guide
And protect you from the hate-rage
Of mankind, I send my light to
Glorify the darkness.

And the rising of the sun shall
Bring forth a brand-new day. The
Thoughts of mankind are evil, but the
Image of God looks down
On Creation in search of peace
And happiness.

In the heart of man
It is brutal; his eye reflects on evil
And his heart is like a pillar
Of stone, ready to conquer the
Weak at his hand.
He shows no mercy. Everyone
In his sight is his enemy.

He has neither strength nor
Spirit; the glory of God
Conquers them all.

PRESSURE

Every day the children cry.
I ask myself the question 'Why?'
Mothers suffer while the fathers die.

The children grow
But as they grow
They have nowhere that they can go.

Society – the strong and mighty keep them down.
Freedom is nowhere to be found.

I see the cruelty of my brothers
And the suffering of my sisters.
Mankind – their hearts are like beasts among the others.

While the leaders sit and watch
Because they like the grief among the others.

My hands are tied,
My feet are bound.
Oh, can I help my brothers' pain and suffering?

I have seen darkness, and
Destruction blocks my way.
Only the strength and determination
Of my heart see me through.

POVERTY

Destruction and poverty
No doctor can cure! I hear
The children crying out for more
Food on their table and love from their parents.

But their parents are nowhere to be
Found. Their fathers are in prison or
In another country fighting wars
For the oppressors of this world.

Their mothers are in the
Rehabilitation centres, sorting out their lives.
You talk about normal life infrastructure
And proper education
While you're building guns and weapons of
Mass destruction to fight against your brothers.

And you leave their children to suffer.
When these children grow up they
Grow up with revenge in their hearts
And more destruction than was ever seen before.

Leaders of this world, control the
Fire before it spreads. Give the
Children what they deserve. And
Unto the fathers and mothers
Let they share the comforts
And joys that life has to offer.

LIKE A RAGING STORM

My love shall never fill with anger,
Destruction or disaster.
It shall be like a flowing stream –
The love and happiness that go through
Your heart.

My love shall be the light
That shines through the darkness
And brings light into your heart.
It shall be the treasure all
Loving arms wish to have.

But the only arms I want are yours.
You are the treasure I choose to have.
In finance nothing compares
To the value of the love I have.

All the riches in the kingdom of the king
(And his treasure is second to none)
Are as nothing to me compared with
The love of your heart.

My kingdom I share and I
Expose my wealth to the
Looter, but the love of my
Lover I would not dispose of or share.

THE VOICE OF MY LOVER

I light a candle to see through
The darkness. I wear sunglasses to
Keep off the glare of the sunlight
But the beauty of my lover
Is second to none.

It is like lying in a dream
That never ends.
The moments seem so true
It is so hard to believe.

To all the ladies: believe me
In what I say. I was there
And I accomplished it.

Let your eyes see and your
Heart accomplish what it needs.

Why does the robin sing in the spring?
The young birds are happy
When the summer comes around,
My darling.

She is like the robin.
She sings to me when I am
Down. And I am like the
Young bird. She brings happiness
To my heart.

TO MANKIND

Many children have never
Seen their father
In the lands they call
Afghanistan, Iraq and Iran.

War is the worst disease
On Planet Earth.
It has no simple cure.
It leaves you with the memory of pain.

She sits there and has nowhere
To go, no food to eat
And no one to talk to –
The lady of the soldier
That fights in the war.

Night and day are just the same:
Pain and anger, sorrow
And frustration.

When the child asks
His mum, "Where is Dad?"
She smiles and says
He is out; he'll soon come back.

THE BEAUTY OF LOVE

Is it a shame
To love the one who loves you
Or cherish the one who cherishes you?
If it is so, then why can't I?
What is more important –
Love or hate?

I climb the hill
To view the valley,
But most interest to me is the valley.
But to see the valley I have to climb
Up the hill.

Happiness lies in one place, but love
Spreads around in many directions.
Like a tree,
There are branches and there are leaves.

There are roots to support
The trunk, and the trunk supports the
Branches, and the branches support the leaves.

Happiness and joy come
When everyone supports each other.
So you see that the hill is important,
Just like the valley.

You're important to me,
Just as I'm important to you.
So that's what I call the
Circle of Love.

The world we are living in – is
It safe? Or is it secure?

Man the leader
Or man the deceiver?
I asked the question,
But the answer was not clear.

So I went on
Seeking to find the truth.
The answers are hidden,
But the seekers are searching.

My Father has created His garden,
And in His garden
There are many things.
He made man to rule over His garden,
But man mismanaged His garden
And friendship broke away.

With love from His heart,
He sent His Son to restore things
And set the record straight.

A saying comes to mind:
'First of all you have to love
Yourself before you can love your
Brothers and sisters.'

Respect yourself
And respect others.

Though a man of any skin colour, race or religion
Can be a good leader,
He must have the right attitude.
He must listen to his people and present
Them with what they need.

But, for me, the true meaning of love
Is togetherness, which means
Sharing and caring.
Like life, it is given and it is taken.

When one is born, another dies.
In everything there is rotation.
One moves and others follow.
Life is unbalanced – we are
Never in the same place all the time.

To get what you want you have to
Strive for it most of the time. Take a chance
And hope for the best.
But to get what you need there is
Nothing much you have to do, because
It is already there. The only thing you
Have to do is take care of it.

What I am talking about is life.
See me – that's what you see.
Hold me – that's what you hold.
Love me – that's what you love.

To be a good father
You must first take care of your
Wife; and in her turn the wife
Takes care of the children.

Then in the house there will always
Be a happy family – like God, our
Heavenly Father.

He provides for us here on earth.
He gives us night to rest and
Day to work and carry on
Our business.

He wants us to respect His
Laws and obey His Commandments
Throughout our life.

We should be like a son or a daughter to.
A good father.

But in life there are many
Ups and downs –
Just like in business –
But we have to move on.

Just like the night to the day,
They accompany each other.
Be strong and have faith in whatsoever you do.

Have hope, and faith will bring success.
Life doesn't guarantee you what you want, but
It gives you what you need. And that
Is life – to carry on.

When life is taken away that is where
It ends for you and me. Remember
I am a poet.

When I am gone my story will always
Be heard, because I am a brother
And also a friend.

I am a servant of the people I
Love and the people I work for.

I am a child of the community
And the charity I work for.
I am a servant of God,
My Holy Father.

I bring news but not riches,
Comfort but not gold.
My brothers, I remind you
To let no one distract you from
The work of your Father.

Take not the inheritance
From thy brother, in case
The fruit you plant shall
Have a bitter taste.

There is a next thing:
Power is given unto the chosen.
Never fight for it,
Because the greed for power
Brings destruction.

Once there was a farmer.
He planted his crop
And there was a long drought,
And he spent his time mumbling.

All of a sudden he got rain,
Which he was praying for.
It brought joy into his heart.

Then the rain continued
And his crop was damaged.
He was so sad in his heart,
But a friend of his came
And said, "Don't worry.

"Pick up what is left and move on.
Pray to God for strength.
He gave you life, so there is hope
Your crop will bear again."

And as he left
The farmer was satisfied.
In a month his crops
Were bearing, and in the harvest
His crop was triple.

My friend, most of the time
Life is not what we want
It to be, but what we need
We receive.

My friend, take a mother
Who carried a child for months
In her womb.
When the child was born she gave
The child away.
Did that mother hate that child?

Some of you would say yes.
In my opinion, the answer is no.
Why? If you hate something,
You destroy it at once.
You wouldn't keep it and
Nurture it and then destroy it.
No, I don't believe it.

But the truth is not only what I believe;
It is what you also believe.
The simple fact is that we are all in
The same corner.

Why? We all rely on our beliefs.
None of us knows what her
Intentions were,
So we rely on our own beliefs.

I believe she gave the child away
So that the child could get a better
Life than the mother could offer.
But sometimes mothers do things in the wrong way
Because the heart of a mother
Rests on the love of her child.
My brother, some of us are
Potential fools.

You may say a
Woman's work is in the house –
The most difficult work,
I think, is in the house
And the most difficult decisions
Are in the house.
There are two houses: there's the
House of importance and the house of decision.
One is run by the man
And the other is run by the woman.
Which one comes out on top?
Have your guess.

One corner is throwing words at
The other, and the other corner
Is dodging the truth, but the survey reveals,
The house of importance, eighty
The house of decision, fifty.

That is why women are very
Important to the future of this world.
Remember, Adam was a lonely
Boy until Eve came by.

I don't say you must give up
Your post, but in that post you
Need help and the input of a
Woman is significant.

Now, my brothers,
Whoever says he knows it all
Knows nothing. He will never
Learn; he will never conceive or receive.
He is an empty plot.

He is like the darkness.
He hides his face from the light
When it presents itself.
He is a lonely soul
Deprived of happiness.

The poet writes.
His heart was full of love;
Then sorrow came by.
I watch the cloud that drifts in the sky
And the vision of my love slowly went by.

My heart was full of grief,
But that was understandable. I sat and wondered,
'What am I going to do?'
For the love of my heart slowly
Departed. The tears from my eyes
I can shed no more.

Oh, can a man grieve for the one
He loves? But he only suffers pain and
Sorrow. The beauty of life never always
Brings happiness;
Only memories remain to those who live
To tell the tale.

Believe in yourself, my brother,
And capture the moment of happiness.
It is true to say that we are required
To love our brother,
But if we don't have love in
Ourselves, how can we love our brother?

Put away your anger for a moment
And try to look for the truth
Within, because your eyes are
Cloudy and your heart is full of
Anger. The true love of your heart
You cannot possess.
My brother, beauty is in your soul
And the stream of love flows
In your heart.

Remove the bitterness from
The taste in your mouth
And the cloud from your eyes.
Let the blind see the richness
And the beauty of the universe.

And with joy the heart shall
Welcome happiness,
And true hearts shall fall in
Love with each other.

Then again, my brother, I went into
Another vision of mine to seek
Glory and overcome sorrow.
There I saw my Master, in whom I trust.

He said, "Come unto Me, all you lost
Sheep that have gone astray.
I shall sacrifice My Son, in whom I
Trust to bring you good tidings.
And on that day you shall rejoice in prayer
With happiness among your brothers
And joy within the hearts of
Your sisters.

Remember Me in sorrow
And rejoice in the time of happiness.
I am the Rock to build upon
And the Foundation that never falls.
I am the Light that shines
Throughout the dark and the Friend
That never departs.

Again I asked myself, 'Why is man
Greedy?' The greed for power
Leads to destruction,
And destruction brings unhappiness.

The man who sets his heart on
Riches and fights for power shall
Also gain destruction.
The bitterness on your tongue shall
Be purged within your belly.

Sugar is sweet, alone or as an
Ingredient, but too much sugar
Can be a disaster to the body.
Fulfil your needs, but do not fill your
Soul with filthiness and destruction.

Godliness is related to cleanliness. Deceive yourself
With pleasure and the wrath of
Your Father shall be upon you. Give me
Strength that I may live and faith
To carry on.

Trouble has fallen upon me. The sorrow
I cannot bear. Love has found me
Wanting. Reach out Your hand and
Lift me up. I am a fallen sheep –
The one that was lost and could not be found.

I search for the light because within
The light I see the truth,
And the truth will satisfy my heart.

The glory of my Father shall shine
Upon me and His blessing shall be overwhelming.
Can a blind man see
Or a deaf man hear?
Most of us are seeing,
But are still blind.

And some of us are hearing but are
Still deaf. Open your eyes and see
The children crying.
They are the future – of tomorrow.

But what kind of future will it be
Without a father to guide them
And a mother to care for them?

Leaders, you are playing with fire,
And fire will burn. Give unto
The fathers and mothers what they
need, and let the children
Share the joy and comfort.

Building more prisons and strengthening the
Army and the air force won't help.
What they need is for us to
Show them love and spend
Some time and listen to their cries.

The toys we buy for birthdays and
Christmas are not what they need;
We must hug them and show them
That we love them.

We spend too much time on the
Stock market or looking at interest
Rates, and we leave our homes to crumble.

Then we try to patch the pieces
When love is all dead. Stop and think.
Spend some time with your family.

To you leaders out there: might
Doesn't beat right. Never make
Decisions in anger; someone will suffer in
The long run. A wise leader listens
To his people.

And discuss matters with the
Leaders of the Churches,
Who are the servants of God.

I tell you, no man is as powerful
As God. He is
Greater than all. I say to you,
Be your brother's keeper
And everlasting peace will lie
In your hearts. I say, no man is
Higher than a mountain and no man
Is lower than the earth.

Be still, my brother, and let the
Light shine through the universe;
And the darkness shall trouble
Not your soul.

Whoever believes in the light
It shall satisfy their heart;
But whoever believes in the darkness
It shall vanish away their soul.

My brother, I believe in the
Pure, for they suffer the most,
Because the pure on earth
Are the poor on earth. They
Have neither silver nor gold,
Nickel nor dime.

But they are the backbone of
The earth. They labour to build
Your castles, and their children go
Into battle and fight wars.

But in old age they end up on
The poverty line with only medals
Of honour to show – and visions
Of the people they killed in
The battles they fought.

If the truth is in you, then
The glory of God shall rise above
Us all and the evil of man
Shall perish like the dust of
The earth we walk upon.

What shall it profit me to
Live in the temple of hell with
All the riches and wealth, the lust
Of the flesh and greed for power?

My brother, this is only a
Moment of happiness in your
Castle of destruction, sorrow and woe.

My brother, lift up yourself
From the sorrow of darkness.
Search for the light, and the
Truth will satisfy your heart.

For the greed for power is
A bellyful of destruction.
My brother, correct me if I'm
Wrong: all humans are brothers and sisters.

Then why can't we live in love
And harmony with each other?
Why do we kill each other and
Then talk about love?

If that is love, then I don't
Want to be involved. I am
Dissatisfied and dejected.
Life is so lonely without love.

So much blood and tears, anger
And destruction! Memories are
Bitter and the future is dark
And disturbing.

Why doesn't the king listen to
The cry of his people? Why is
The food of his people given
To the dog and the swine?
Why is the heart of man so corrupt?

I speak not just for myself
But for others around me –
The ones that work from sunup
Until sundown and get
Just a nickel and a dime.

Their children don't see any
Future in themselves, but you
Are the one that spends millions
On weapons, killing off
Others in the name of power
And greed.

Meanwhile, the elderly people, who
Are the backbone of the
Country can't even afford
A glass of milk or a
Loaf of bread. But remember: no
One is born old. Life is a
Blessing, but some men pray that they will
Never grow old
Or feel the pinch of what some
Of my sisters and brothers went through.

It is an honour to be brave and
Strong, but it is a disgrace to
Turn your back on your suffering brothers.

Help the weak if you are
Strong. Unto the poor you give
Bread. Lead the blind
Because you can see. If they
Stumble, give them a helping hand.

Remember: don't give in to what
The world desires. Lust and vanity
Lead to destruction,
Evil and corruption. Be of good
Faith and fear no one. Walk in
The path of righteousness and you
Shall overcome evil.

Be yourself and grudge not your
Brother for his wealth or his
Woman. Give thanks for what you
Achieve. With hard work
And good planning you will achieve your goal.

Remember, brothers: there were many
Before you, and there will be many after you.
You are in the middle, so don't waste time.

There might never be another chance.
Who knows if the sun will shine
Tomorrow or the stars will shine in
The sky tonight?

My brothers, don't be deceived by
Man or by what you see, because in
Everything there is a season.

A time for joy
And a time for sorrow.

A time for work
And a time for play.

A time for love
And a time for hate.

A time for war
And a time for peace.

The season and the time
No man can change.
I like to be free,
But I am in darkness.

My heart is full of hate-rage
And my eyes are full of
Darkness. I am looking, but I am
Blind. I have no vision of my own.

Suddenly I rise from my dream
And beside me is my lover.
I say to her, "Grant a wish
To me before I die."
She says to me, "Your wish
Is my command."

Then she sings
Like the robin that sings in
The morning. Her voice is like
A violin or a trumpet that
Blows in heaven, and the beautiful
Angels gather around to
Sing the morning chorus
To the master of the ceremony.

I open my eyes and joy fills
My heart with the beauty of
Your love. You comfort me with the
Charm of your happiness.

I walk the Valley of Unhappiness
When I see the dark side of life
And when I see the suffering of my
Brothers and sisters –
Those who have no joy to share,
But only bitterness and sad stories.
I say to myself, "What can I
Do to satisfy my heart with
The love and happiness I long to share?"

I need not this sorrow. It is too
Hard for me to bear.
I wish to see the beauty
Of love and the time of joy
When you and I can sit and share.

Oh, life is more precious
Than silver and gold!
Oh, the dreams we have
And the laughter we share!

Oh, I sit in the moonlight
With happiness going through my heart,
I sit and wonder about the
Days when love was true.

It was like honey to the lips
And the blood that serves
The heart. Like the wise men
Say, knowledge can increase
Bitterness and bitterness can be
A purge to your belly.

In the darkness I light my
Candle, and in the light I fear
No darkness.
Walk with me hand in hand,
And let us view the beauty of this land,
Float in the sea and play in the sand.

It is many years since we were children.
The glory days have passed and gone.
But remember the rising sun
That brings the dawn.

Seasons come and seasons go
But the beauty of love will always flow.